Table of Contents

Introduction

This book contains words and names based on original Hebrew. When I say "original," I am referring to the original and first language that the Scriptures were written in. Before you continue reading this book I would like to go over some of the words used.

Jew - Many find the words in Hebrew too "Jewish," but I assure you they are not. Let me start by explaining the term "Jew." The term "Jew" and "Judaism" come from Judah. Judah was the fourth son of Jacob, who later became known as Israel. The Hebrew word for Judah is "Yehudah" and it means "Praise."

King David and King Solomon were both from the tribe of Yehudah, as was the Messiah, Jesus, or Yeshua. When Solomon died around 925 BCE (Before the Common Era), there were ten tribes that would not submit to his son Rehoboam as King. From this, the tribes were split into two kingdoms; the north (Israel) and the south (Judah). The southern kingdom contained the tribes of Yehudah (Judah) and Benyamin (Benjamin) which can mean either "Son of the south" or "Son of the right hand." There were also some Levites and priests among them. The southern kingdom was centered around Jerusalem (Yerushalem) and the Temple.

In the 5th century BCE, the Assyrian king Sennaherib came against the northern kingdom where they were dispersed and exiled. The southern kingdom remained (known as the Kingdom of Yehudah) and would come to be known as the Yehudi, or "Jews."

Yeshua - Do you remember the bracelets everyone used to wear that had "WWJD" on them for "What Would Jesus Do"? I believe that it should actually be "WWYD" for "What Would Yeshua Do."

In Matthew 1:21, the Angel Gavriel (Gabriel) states,

> "And she shall bring forth a son, and you shall call His name JESUS: for he will save His people from their sins." (NKJV)

In Hebrew, as I will explain more in chapter 2, this sentence is a Hebrew word pun. He says, "You shall call his name Yeshua (salvation): for he shall Yoshia (save) his people from their sins."

Gavriel would have been speaking in Hebrew because the Yehudi (Jewish) people, Miriam (Mary) and Yoseph (Joseph) were Yehudi (Jews). They were Hebrew reading, writing and speaking people within a Hebrew culture and society. So if they wrote up birth certificates in those days, his would certainly say under the name section "Yeshua Ben Yoseph" or "Yeshua son of Joseph."

Yeshua's name has gone through quite a change over the centuries. Though there are many theories, this is mine.

3

Yeshua in Hebrew is spelled as יֵשׁוּעַ. The Greek had changed it to meet their language standards, however they did not have any equivalent to the Hebrew "Yod" (which is equivalent to the modern English "Y"), so they used Iota-Epsilon (IE) though some translate it with Iota-Eta (IH). They also did not have anything to make the "sh" sound, so it was then made into a Sigma (Σ). The following letters were to meet the closest sound as well as the Greek rules for masculine names, which were Upsilon-Sigma (ΥΣ) or a possible Omicron-Upsilon-Sigma (ΟΥΣ). Greek masculine names would add a Sigma to the end of the name making such names like Moshe into Moses.

The name took on the form of either ΙΗΣΟΥΣ or ΙΕΣΟΥΣ or ΙΕΣΥΣ, causing the pronunciation "Iesous."

The King James translators used a collection of Greek manuscripts to create their version of the Bible. Going from Greek then Latin to Old-English. Generally, the pronunciation is the same, "Iesous." Eventually though the "I" would be split into "I" and "J" and the "O" was dropped from the name. They would keep the "J" form, which for a time still held the "Y" sound but eventually would become what we know today to have the "J" sound, thus ending with "Jesus."

My name is Michael. If you were to translate my name into other languages the pronunciation would change. In Hebrew it is Mihaal, Japanese is Mikaru, Spanish is Miguel and in French it is Michel. However, if I were to go to any of these countries I would prefer my name be what it has been all my life and says on my birth certificate; "Michael." I am not saying that the name of "Jesus" is wrong to use, but for me it is "Yeshua," and I believe he would want things to stay original and as close to the roots as possible. So, "WWYD" is what I would say.

If you were to go to Israel and ask the following questions, the outcome would be the same.

1. *Do all Hebrew names have a meaning?*

   Answer: Yes

2. *What does Jesus mean?*

   Answer: Nothing, it's not a Hebrew name.

3. *What does Yeshua mean?*

   Answer: Salvation.

For me, and my walk, I choose to use the name that has meaning.

Now I will examine some other words that require less of an explanation.

Tanakh/Tanak – An acrostic referring to the Old Testament. It is made up of the words "Torah," "Nevi'im" and "Ketuvim."

Torah – Instructions/Law

Nevi'im – Prophets

Ketuvim - Writings

Torah – Instructions; also translated as "Law." This is a reference to the first five books of Scripture – Genesis, Exodus, Leviticus, Numbers and Deuteronomy.

Genesis = Barashite, meaning "In the beginning."

Exodus = Shemot/Sh'mot, meaning "Names."

Leviticus = Vayikra, meaning "And he called."

Numbers = Bamidbar, meaning "In the desert [of]."

Deuteronomy = Devarim, meaning "[Spoken] Words."

B'rit Chadesha – Term used for the New Testament meaning Renewed/New Covenant.

Hebrew - From the word "Avrit" meaning to "Cross over". It is the idea of crossing over from paganism into the ways of God.

Elohim – Term often used for God. Can also be El or Eloi. Eloi is equal to saying "My God."

Yah – A poetic short form of the Creator's Name. This will be discussed further in chapter 6.

Halleluyah/Hallelujah – Praise be unto Yah.

There are other Hebrew words used within this book, but I will go into more detail of those when they are introduced later in this book.

Author's Note

"Now when they saw the boldness of Peter and John, and perceived that they were uneducated and untrained men, they marveled. And they realized that they had been with Jesus/Yeshua." (Acts 4:13)

This is how I want to be known. Can you imagine talking to someone, just you with the Spirit/Ruach, and that person marvels at your words realizing that you had been with Yeshua? I like to think about Peter, how he was a simple fisherman and became an Apostle for the Messiah. His training? He walked with Yeshua. No classes, no seminary, no special training or education - he simply walked with Yeshua.

I, like Peter, have never had any official training or education outside of a High School diploma. I became a children's church minister, then a youth pastor in 2 different churches, a worship band member and used to hold Bible studies in my home. What made me qualified? Nothing, in the eyes of man, I had never been licensed to minister. But I did have the Scriptures available to me, and enough resources to study the Hebrew language, the Hebrew culture, and their history from the beginning until now.

I felt compelled to write this book, to deliver a message into your hands. The message of the book itself is reason enough.

However, I also wanted to show fellow believers that they do not need anything more than the Scriptures and a relationship with the Creator. We can take the message of the Kingdom to the world without needing seminary or Bible classes. Yeshua said he would send us the Ruach to lead us into all Truth. Though I do acknowledge the necessity of teachers and other programs, I believe strongly that just as Peter and John were untrained and uneducated, we too today, can do great and mighty things.

But the main reason I wrote this book, is because there seems to be something not quite right. Not that everyone is doing everything wrong, but it seems that many are doing almost nothing that the Messiah told us to be doing. Sure, we accept Yeshua as our Savior, but do we walk His walk, or do we just talk the talk? I address these things in this book.

I believe the material in this book will give believers a more solid stance on why we do what we do. Then, I send out a call to get back on the path that was laid out for us to walk. We may stray sometimes, it happens, but I am here to say, it's time to get back on the path.

What is it that truly matters when it comes down to it? I don't care what we call ourselves - Messianic, Hebrew Roots, Torah-Keepers, etc. We all want to find out the Truth and walk in that Truth. In order to do so, we need to return to the basics, or the root of the Scriptures. Once we are back on the path, I believe we can then share the Truth and help others onto the path and to stay on the path.

Shalom/Peace.

Chapter 1 – The Problem

There is a passage I have read many times. And I have spent many sleepless nights dwelling on it. Frankly, it disturbed me. These words were written down as part of an historic account of a man who walked the Earth around 2000 years ago. His name is Yeshua. Most people know him as Jesus. I used to call him that; but I found the more I studied and researched the Scriptures and their histories, I began calling him Yeshua. I will go further into this later; but for now, I want to focus on His words.

Yeshua spoke these words near the end of a sermon He spoke on a mountain. After a few pages and chapters of reading the red letters that represent Yeshua's words in my NKJV Bible, I finally came across this part of the passage. It's a familiar passage that begins with what has been deemed "The Beatitudes." And it is this passage that caused my uneasiness. It says:

"Not everyone who says to me, 'Lord, Lord,' shall enter the kingdom of Heaven, but he who does the will of my Father in Heaven. Many will say to me in that day, 'Lord, Lord,

have we not prophesied in your name, cast out demons in your name and done many wonders in your name?' And then I will declare to them, 'I never knew you; depart from me, you who practice lawlessness!'"
(NKJV)

The passage is found in Matthew 7:21-23. The fact that it was written by Matthew is an important matter, which I will cover later in this book.

Let's examine each line. The first being, "Not everyone who says to me, 'Lord, Lord,' shall enter the kingdom of Heaven." I want to talk about these words from the point of view of an English speaking man who is writing to an audience of English speaking people. We will delve more into other languages later.

I will rephrase what Yeshua says here, "Not everyone who says to me 'Lord, Lord' is getting in." This can be a scary thought if examined long enough. How many of us have called Yeshua or His Father "Lord"? I know I certainly have. And yet, he seems to say here that calling him "Lord" does not earn you a place in Heaven. This reminds me of another passage later in the New Testament, also known as the B'rit Chadesha in Hebrew meaning "Renewed Covenant."

"That if you confess with your mouth the Lord Jesus and believe in your heart that

10

God has raised Him
from the dead, you
will be saved."

Romans 10:9 (NKJV)

These words were written by Paul. Maybe he never read the book of Matthew because he seems to be saying that if you confess Yeshua as "Lord" you can be saved. Of course, there is another part of the statement here, "...and believe in your heart that God has raised Him from the dead, you will be saved." So maybe the people Yeshua was talking about didn't believe. Could that be the issue? But then I'm reminded of something James said:

"You believe that
there is one God.
You do well. Even
the   demons
believe—and
tremble!"

James 2:19 (NKJV)

Maybe even belief isn't enough? Though this could just be semantics. James, (who in Hebrew is Ya'akov which means "Jacob," not James) seems to be saying that belief isn't enough, but then, he could just be talking about belief in one God. We could be onto something here, but let's move on.

Yeshua could just be saying that they call him "Lord" without the belief. Or, maybe he is saying something more than that. The word "Lord," believe it or not, is a very hot topic. Many disagree that Yeshua or even his Father should be called "Lord." There are several arguments for both sides. One is that Ba'al means "Lord" or "Master." Ba'al is a pagan, false god, found in the Old Testament (or Tanakh – as previously discussed, an

11

acronym for Torah, Nevi'im and Ketuvim). There are many references to Ba'al including Elijah (Eliyahu), who called fire from Heaven using the true name of the Almighty God (or El) and defeated the prophets of Ba'al on top of a mountain. So the argument is that because this false god was known as "Lord," we should not call the Almighty "Lord." Ba'al is also part of a title attributed to Satan (Hebrew for "Adversary") known as Ba'alzebub, which means "Lord of the flies."

Another issue however, is that Adonai is another Hebrew term which means "Lords," but is constantly attributed to the Almighty God throughout the Hebrew Scriptures. This is a tricky subject to explain, but I will do my best.

Back several centuries ago, there was a ban on the use of the name of the Almighty God. It was deemed by religious leaders as "too holy" to pronounce, and therefore ineffable. So within the Scriptures, the holy Name was replaced with Adonai, when referring to the Almighty. They also used the term Hashem (The Name). In most English translations today, any time you see in all capital letters "LORD" or "GOD," this is where the true Name would have originally been written, but was then hidden.

Adoni and Adonai come from the singular form "Adon," meaning "Lord" or "Owner." Adoni claims "My Lord" and Adonai claims "My Lords." So then, the argument comes in that, since the true Name was concealed using Adonai, we should not call him this. I disagree.

Adonai was used in the Scriptures in places other than when covering up "The Name." I think, if the writers of the Scriptures were commanded by the Almighty to write certain things, and because they felt inspired to use them, it is perfectly fine to call Him Adoni, Adon, LORD! And to call Yeshua "Lord," is also permissible since He has been exalted to the right hand of authority next to the Father. We should also call the Almighty by His Name; but I will be getting into that later.

With this in mind, I don't believe the issue is found within calling Yeshua "Lord" or simply not believing. I think there is more to this than all of that, which is why context is essential in finding out anything stated in Scripture. Now we will examine the next line.

"...But he who does the will of my Father in Heaven." Okay, so maybe the issue is resolved. In simple terms, Yeshua is basically saying that not everyone who says to him "Lord, Lord" gets into Heaven, but whoever does what his Father wants done will get in.

The issue was not that everyone who claims Yeshua as Lord (or at least calls him Lord) gets into Heaven, but whoever does what his Father wants them to do. Problem solved, right? I don't think so. Look at what Yeshua goes on to say in the next line.

"Many will say to me in that day, 'Lord, Lord, have we not prophesied in your name, cast out demons in your name, and done many wonders in your name?'" These people, whoever they are, are pleading for their lives by telling Yeshua all the things they did. They seem to have been doing the will of the Father! At least, that's what it sounds like. They prophesied, they cast out demons and they even did many wonders; all in the name of Yeshua. Isn't that the will of the Father? Well, we have one more line that says otherwise.

"And then I will declare to them, 'I never knew you; depart from me, you who practice lawlessness!'" The problem just got a whole lot more complex and frankly, downright scary. These people sounded like they did some amazing things. They sound like several televangelists I've seen on T.V. and in live sessions. Is

13

it me or does something seem a little off? What is Yeshua saying here?

Let's sum this chapter up. Not everyone who says "Lord" gets into Heaven; but you get in if you do what the Father wants. Even if you prophesy, cast out demons and do many wonders, you're STILL going to be told that Yeshua doesn't know you and to leave! He then called them lawbreakers, saying 'you who practice lawlessness!'

I know how it all seems - contradicting and hopeless. Can anyone get into Heaven at all? Believe it or not, the answer is yes.

Earlier in this chapter, I mentioned context. Context, when studying Scripture, is critical! You won't understand Revelation unless you read Genesis. You won't get Matthew if you don't read Exodus. You won't even truly get the first five books of Scripture unless you read the rest of Scripture, or the rest of Scripture unless you read the first five books! I'm going to try to put these three verses into a contextual perspective for you and explain how they are probably some of the most important words Yeshua ever spoke and how they are still relevant for all believers today.

The key to answering the question is found in the very last line: "I never knew you; depart from me, you who practice lawlessness!" This book will be focused on getting to know Yeshua and understanding what practicing lawlessness means. Along the way, I want to explain some other things, like the name of God, who Yeshua really is and what being a true believer and follower should look like. By the end of the book, we are not only going to know what it looks like; we are going to look like it!

Chapter 2 – The Torah and the Messiah

This chapter will touch on many different topics. The goal however, is that by the end of the chapter, you will hopefully see that they all come together to complete a single concept. Like, several threads coming together, to form a beautiful bow.

I'm going to start with something that I am very passionate about and is key to everything; Truth.

TRUTH

Truth is defined by Webster's Online Dictionary as:

n 1 – The quality of being true; as:
(a) Conformity to fact or reality; exact accordance with that which is, or has been; or shall be.

This very definition greatly interests me. First of all, I see the "n." for noun. I remember in Elementary school learning that a noun is either a "person, place or a thing." What's fun about what we are dealing with in this book, is in this case – Truth, is all three.

What is truth? Truth is true, fact and reality. Another word I would like to use to describe it, is that it, is just awesome. Like the law of gravity, it cannot be changed. If you jump off a house, you will hit the ground. Another attribute of truth, is that, it is absolute. Truth is not relative.

Many argue that it is relative. That, "What is true for you is not true for me." This only works in petty circumstances. I can state in truth that, "I am a man." This is true for me but not true for my wife. She cannot truthfully state that she is a man. But we are not here to deal with the small and petty matters; we are here to deal with Truth in its enormity.

I have heard many non-believers say that truth is relative and that there is no absolute truth, to which I like to respond, "Is that absolutely true?" While this can be a hard philosophical idea to wrestle with, the truth is, that we human beings are finite and do not have the capacity to deal with the absolute in its grand scale of truth and intensity.

It boils down to one reason, and the reason I'd like to discuss in this section is that Truth is a person.

While it is fun to see the Webster definition of Truth and the opinions that come with it, what I'm really interested in talking about is WHO Truth is.

Let me pause briefly, just to say this. Remember, these are all separate topics we will be going over, but my hope is that by the end of this chapter, it will all come together as a single topic. And before jumping to any conclusions, I will go ahead and state that I am not giving an affirmation for or against the doctrine of the Trinity. That is not my goal in this book. The goal of this book is exactly what I said at the end of the first chapter, and that is what we will be focusing on.

אמת/Emet/Truth

The word is just as beautiful in Hebrew as it is in English. Truth has been with us since the beginning. It has traveled through time and will be far in the future. In talking about Truth as a person, I want to do so by examining a few verses from the Scriptures that deal with who Truth is.

> Yeshua said to him, "I am the way, the truth, and the life. No one comes to the Father, except through me."
>
> John 14:6 (HNV)

Yeshua made a very bold claim here. He claims to be the Truth. But he also attributes himself to being the way and the life. These three seem to be synonymous. If you walk in "the way," then you are in "the truth" which in turn seems also to be the very essence of "the life" but also leads to "the life."

So what else is true in Scripture?

> "You are near, O YHVH, and all Your Commandments are truth."
>
> Psalm 119:151 (HNV)
>
> "But let YHVH be true, and every man false."
>
> Romans 3:4a (HNV)

17

The Psalmist states that the Commandments are true. The Almighty first spoke these words in Exodus, or Shemot (meaning Names). The first Ten Commandments were spoken and later written by the Almighty. This is found in the Torah, meaning "Instructions," which are the first five books of the Bible in the Old Testament, or Tanakh. It is later stated in Romans, a New Testament/B'rit Chadesha writing, to be true. As the Almighty said through Balaam in Numbers/Bamidbar 23:19, "God is not man, that He should lie, or a son of man, that he should change His mind." This gives weight to my previous statement that truth is Absolute.

I want to focus on the Commandments. The Torah, more specifically, are the Instructions for the people of the Almighty to live their lives by. You could say that this is "The Way." Interestingly, the final book of the Torah, Deuteronomy, is called in Hebrew "Devarim," meaning "[Spoken] Words." The Torah is the Word of God that Yeshua spoke about while being tempted when he said, "Man shall not live by bread alone, but by every Word that proceeds out of the mouth of YHVH," which he quoted directly from Deuteronomy/Devarim 8:3.

This reminds me, and possibly you, of the book of John/Yochanon 1:1, which says:

> "In the beginning was the Word, and the Word was with Elohim, and the Word was Elohim."
>
> John 1:1 (HRB)

Let's recap before we move on to the next topic. Yeshua said he is the way, the truth and the life. The way is the Torah which is also the Word of God, which is true, having come from the Almighty who does not lie. Now look at John/Yochanon 1:14,

"The Word became flesh." It is revealed that Yeshua is the Word. Man lives by every word that comes from the Almighty. It is most interesting to see all of these things coming into oneness, and we're not even finished yet!

מלה/Milah /Word

Now I would like to focus in more detail on the Word aspect of Yeshua. Seeing as there does not seem to be any Hebrew manuscripts that we know of for John, I think it would be a safe assumption that the word for "Word" in Hebrew is "Milah" or "Dabar/Davar."

These words both mean "word," but in different ways. Depending on the context they can mean either the written word or the spoken word. "Davar" is typically used for the spoken word, while "Milah" is often used in general for "word." In Genesis/Barashite 15:1, it says that "The Word (Davar) of YHVH came to Avraham in a vision."

In John 1, the theme of the Word comes into play. The Word isn't simply a word but a person, even so far as to say "God Himself." Oneness with God is key, but in what way? Is this to say that the Word is the Almighty God Himself? I think this can be true, but is also something else. As previously mentioned, Yeshua is revealed to be the Word. The Word is more than it, or he, seems.

Throughout Scripture, the Word is Law. It is whatever the Almighty speaks. It is true. Whenever a Prophet spoke, Scripture will use a phrase like, "The Word of YHVH came upon..." In Numbers/Bamidbar 23, Balaam was said to have had a "Word (Davar) put in his mouth." Even though Balaam turned out to be a false man, when the Almighty spoke through him, Balaam had no other choice but to speak the truth that had come from Him.

Therefore, the Word is most certainly what comes from the Almighty. He speaks and thus it is the Word.

The Torah was first spoken. This is important because as you can see in Exodus 20, the Almighty began to speak the first of the Commandments to the Hebrew People. Once He had reached the tenth, the people shouted out in fear begging to never hear the voice of God again, lest they should die, but instead that it be told to Moses/Moshe, that he may deliver to them the Word that comes from God. The Almighty agreed to this, though if you read before this occured, He knew this would happen all along. Thus the Torah was written, but was first, spoken. We may also consider that the Universe and the Earth were created with spoken words/Devarim.

The book of Deuteronomy in Hebrew is called Devarim, which means "[Spoken] Words." This book is somewhat of a recap of the Torah. Rightly so, it is also the last of the five books that make up the entire Torah. So the spoken Word of the Almighty became written down and passed on from one generation to the next, and so forth, and is accepted by the People of God as the Word of God. Isaiah/Yeshayahu said it right and Peter repeated it, that the words of God endure forever.

Next, as the Word is still accepted as the Torah and the spoken words from God, we have a new layer of Truth to it. John 1 will be key in this.

John states that the Word was in the Beginning. It almost appears to be a mirrored wording from Genesis/Barashite 1. The Word was in the Beginning and was with God and was God. Would it be that God's Word is equal to He, Himself as True and Good; to disobey His Words would be to disobey the Almighty Himself? I think the answer can only be yes. So then, His Word is Himself also.

20

All things were made through, and by the Word (V. 3) and in the Word was life (V. 4) and that life was the light of man. The Word is a big deal.

Later in verse 14, the Word became flesh and dwelt among us. Interestingly, some translations say the Word became flesh and "tabernacled" among us. We will examine this in a later chapter as well.

So then, that Word (that became flesh) is Yeshua. What could this mean? Does this mean to say that Yeshua is a man made out of words? Can you look at his face and see written text? Most likely, not. Therefore, there must be a deeper meaning. Granted, many have sought to interpret this text's meaning, and our examination is no different. But my hope is that by the end of this chapter, we will have a further understanding of the person of Yeshua.

Yeshua is the Word made into man. Synonymously, Yeshua is the Word that John 1 describes. Yeshua was a perfect, sinless man. That is what the New Testament refers to him as; spotless, blameless, sinless and without fault. He describes himself as "The Way, the Truth and the Life." A play on words could be when he says, "No one can come to the Father but by me." If you look at the fact that John 1 states that "All things were made through the Word," it's true, had we not been made by the Word, it would be impossible to approach the Father! Again, the Word is a big deal!

Yeshua's way of life was the Torah. As a Jew and a Hebrew, he taught and interpreted the Torah. When tempted by Satan he always responded with, "It is written..." and quoted the Word of God. It is what was expected of him as a servant and follower of the Torah of God, and he walked it perfectly to his death.

The Word is described as life, and that life, being the light of man. Light reveals truths hidden in the dark. The Pharisees of Yeshua's time, and in today's time, had what they called Takanot. It was false 'oral regulations' said to have been given along with the written Torah. Any time you see Yeshua being scolded by the Pharisees for "breaking the rules," it was one of their own man-made rules, or Takanot. Yeshua followed one Torah; the Torah of God. This frustrated the Pharisees and they saw that as he was perfect in the Father's will and Torah. Therefore, not wanting that they should give up their high status as religious leaders, they sought to kill him. This being said, the light of the Word exposed them for who they truly were.

Briefly, I want to explain something many call the "Hebrew Matthew." A scroll was found some time ago, of the gospel of Matthew, written in Hebrew rather than Greek. This is important for several reasons. One major reason is that we found that some things Yeshua said were worded differently than in the Greek translation, and though it was a word here or there, they were very big differences, because the words have different meanings in Hebrew than they do in Greek.

In Matthew 23:2, which was translated from Greek, Yeshua says that "The Scribes and Pharisees sit in Moshe's seat, therefore whatever they tell you to observe, that observe and do..."

In the Hebrew Matthew it says, "Therefore whatever HE tells you to observe, that observe and do..." Who is "he"? Moshe! Moses. Yeshua in fact said, to obey the Torah and its commandments, which were written by Moshe with the anointing of the Almighty. Let's continue.

After Yeshua's death and resurrection, he explained to the disciples, how the events that took place were fulfillments of the Word of God (or Scriptures). They then saw and understood that

22

everything that had happened was planned from the very beginning.

In summary to this topic, Yeshua walked, talked, breathed and fulfilled the Word. He was and is the encapsulation, the very essence and being of the Word. In fact, Yeshua said in John 5:19:

> "Most certainly, I tell you, the son can do nothing of himself, but what he sees the Father doing. For whatever things He does, these the son also does likewise."
> (HNV)

I would like to submit that Yeshua, being the Word, was and is the will of the Father incarnate. He was the essence of His voice, the actions of His Words, the Dictionary, the Thesaurus, the Encyclopedia and the very Word itself, or Himself, walking among the people and whoever desired to know more stayed by his side. Yeshua taught the Word as a living, breathing and walking Mount Moriah; Yah (poetic short form of the Father's name) is our Moreh (teacher).

I'll be honest, that I have never heard anyone refer to Yeshua as "Mount Moriah." I was sitting and thinking about the different things I would go over in this book and upon meditating on the idea of who Truth is, being Yeshua, this one thought had entered my mind. Once it did, it never left. And so, this is our next topic.

מוֹרִיָּה/**Moriah**

It was interesting to me to find that the name "Moriah" was only mentioned in Scripture two times; once in Genesis/Barashite and the other in 2 Chronicles. Genesis/Barashite 22:2 reads:

> "And He said, 'Now take your son, Isaac, your only one whom you love, and go into the land of Moriyah. And there offer him for a burnt offering on one of the mountains which I will say to you.'" (HNV)

This is an all too familiar story. Abraham/Avraham is told by the Almighty to take his son Isaac to a designated place to be sacrificed by Avraham's own hand. The whole time, Avraham maintains his faith that a sacrifice will be provided. Just before carrying out the sacrificing of his son, a voice shouts out to Avraham to stop and a Ram was provided instead. I have heard and read from several sources, and I agree, that this was a type and shadow, or a type of example, of the Messiah's crucifixion on the cross.

The only other time Moriah is mentioned is in 2 Chronicles 3:1 which states:

> "And Solomon began to build the house of YHVH at Jerusalem, in Mount Moriyah,

24

where He appeared to his father David, in the place that David had prepared, in the grain floor of Ornan the Jebusite." (HNV)

This is the building of the Temple. So much significance is held in this location. Many speculate as well that this may be the very same place Avraham had taken Isaac as instructed by the Almighty. However, this would be the place where the Temple was built, the place it is said that Yah would be our Moreh; our Teacher.

Mount Zion was just south of Moriah. Zion would become where the royal residence was. The Ark of the Covenant was of course within the Temple until it was transferred to the royal residence. Eventually the two terms "Holy Mountain" and "Zion" would be used to describe the entire area we know as Jerusalem.

Jerusalem's meaning is somewhat of a mystery. Having several opinions of the meaning, the two that are more accepted are "City of Peace" and the possible "Foundation of God." These two certainly make sense if you refer to Yeshua as Moriah, for within the Word, light, truth and life of God you most certainly find peace (Shalom). Also, considering the Torah to be the instructions or Law of the Almighty, it is the Foundation to the whole of the Scriptures. I found a verse that best words what I am trying to express, Psalm 89:14:

"Justice and righteousness are Your throne's foundation; mercy

and truth go before
Your face." (HRB)

Justice and righteousness cannot be found where there is
no law to compare to. Imagine you are driving down the road and
you are driving at 70 MPH. The speed limit is 45 MPH. According
to the law, should you be brought to justice? If the law says so,
then yes! Most people would receive a speeding ticket. But
imagine if there was no law. Then there would be no speed limit
of 45 MPH. Therefore, there is no cause for justice. Do you see
how it works? The law forbids that we drive faster than the speed
limit given, so then, we ought to obey the law which makes us by
definition RIGHTEOUS! But if you were to break that law by
driving faster than the speed limit, then, you would deserve
justice. We want to be a people of righteousness. Consider also
that Yeshua is of the order of Melchizedek. Melchizedek means
"King of Righteousness." I will explain this in more detail later in
this book.

My perspective of "Moriah" is that it is the "Mountain that
Yah teaches from." The assembly, sacrifices; all of this historically
happened in that place, and our appointed times (Moedim) to
meet with Him were numerous on that mountain. Therefore, I
believe that we should let the Messiah, our very own Mount
Moriah and Melchizedek, teach us His ways as they are the
foundation to everything.

ודרך חיים/The Way and The Life

While this topic will deal with the aspects of the Way and
the Life, I want to begin by talking about the name of the Messiah;
Yeshua.

26

Yeshua in Hebrew means "Salvation." However, this is not the only version of his name that believers use. "Yeshua" is the version I use because of the passage from Matthew 1:21:

> "And she will bear a son, and you shall call His name Yeshua, for He shall save His people from their sins." (HRB)

This type of statement can be found throughout Scripture. They are popularly called "Hebraisms." Hebraisms are like idioms. You cannot find it in English, but in Hebrew it would be like saying, "You shall call his name Yeshua, for he shall yoshia his people from their sins." Yeshua can mean "salvation," "to rescue" or "to deliver." Yoshia means "save." So the idiom, or Hebraism, can be found by saying, "You shall call his name Salvation, for he shall save his people from their sins." Another example from Genesis/Barashite, Adam came from the Adamah, or ground.

Other forms of his name can be Yehshua, Yahshua and Yehoshua. Yehshua and Yahshua are popularized determining on what the user's preference is of God's Name, either Yahweh or Yehovah (or other versions I'll discuss later in this book). Yah is a poetic short form of the Creator's name, like we see in the phrase "HalleluYah." Together with "Yeshua" the name then would mean, "Yah is salvation."

Yehoshua is Hebrew for "Joshua." It holds the same meaning, as "Yah is salvation." The other versions of the name are shortened versions. All of them are based more or less on personal preference and I have no quarrel with anyone's use of them, as long as they know the "who" rather than simply the name.

Salvation is the key here. The way to life is through Salvation, or, the way to life is through Yeshua.

In the same chapter that this book started with I found Yeshua saying something quite sobering to the idea of the "Way" and "Life." In Matthew 7:13-14 Yeshua states:

> "Go in through the narrow gate; for wide is the gate and broad is the way that leads to destruction, and many are the ones entering in through it.
>
> For narrow is the gate, and constricted is the way that leads away into life, and few are the ones finding it." (HRB)

Though this is self-explanatory, I still have to ask what the "way" is that he is referring to here. I think, again, the answer is found in the latter verse. The way that leads to destruction would be the way of lawlessness (or being without Torah; Torahlessness). The way that leads away into life would be the Torah.

I believe the evidence is found in Psalm/Tehellim 119:105 which states, "Your Word is a lamp to my feet and a light to my path." Psalm 119 is a poem involving every letter of the Hebrew alphabet, or "alephbet." It is the longest chapter in all of Scripture and is about the beauty of the Torah.

In Summary, Yeshua is the way, the truth and the life. None come to the Father but by Him. This is to say that belief in Yeshua is critical. Not only that, He is the Messiah, but in that He is the Torah and his very example is the way of life which can be found in the Torah as well as the fact that the Torah and Prophets speak of Him in prophecy.

His every word and every action were because the Father willed it. He did nothing unless the Father did and said nothing unless the Father said.

Truth cannot fail. Yeshua's death and resurrection, though having many reasons for having taken place, give validity or authority to this fact. By his death and resurrection we were made his righteousness. We were also grafted in to the covenant the Almighty had made with His people which is basically that if we obey His commands, He will bless us (Leviticus/Vayikra 26). But also, because Yeshua, the Truth, resurrected, we know, that Truth as a person and as an idea cannot be done away with. Truth reigns! If Yeshua, who is Truth and the Word, resurrected from the grave (as the Scriptures prophesied that he would in Psalm 16:9-11) then Truth cannot be destroyed.

The Torah, the Word of God, leads us in every way of life. Stray from it or reject it and we may find only death and destruction. In the Word was found light, which was the life of man, and that light is what shows us the path beneath our feet. If we are walking in Torah, as Yeshua walked and taught, then our result, unquestionably, is life.

If we are in obedience to the Word, the Torah of God, then we are also inside the will of love. God is love; therefore His words are also love. God's will is love.

Yeshua said in John 5:46:

> "For if you believed
> Moses, you would
> believe me; for he
> wrote of me."
> (HNV)

Yeshua is the Way, the Truth and the Life. None come to the Father but by Yeshua, but by Salvation, but by Torah, but by Love.

Chapter 3 – The Anti-Torah and the Anti-Messiah

This chapter deals with the rebellion against the Almighty and His Torah. Before we get into this, I want to talk about Yeshua as the Messiah, first. You may wonder why I didn't talk about this in the previous chapter. My reason is because I want to show more side-by-side comparisons of what the Messiah of God looks like when compared to that of an anti-messiah.

מ‎שיח/Mashiach/Messiah

Mashiach means "anointed" or "anointed one." Commonly the Messiah is referred to as "Christ" in North America as well as other places around the world. I use the term Messiah for several reasons.

Messiah is more closely related to the Hebrew term "Mashiach." Seeing as the Messiah was, or is, a Hebrew man, this version seems to make the most sense.

"Christ" originates from the Greek version of this term which is "Christos." I don't have any personal discrepancies with anyone who uses the term "Christ," nor do I have any real problems with the term itself. However, as you have probably already noticed from reading thus far, I tend to favor the Hebrew terms. My reasoning is that if our Creator chose to be the God of a Hebrew group of people, and His Scriptures were written in Hebrew as well as His people spoke in the Hebrew language, as His Messiah is a Hebrew, then for me the obvious choice is to use the Hebrew and refer to it more than the Greek.

Although there is evidence that most of the New Testamen/B'rit Chadesha was originally written in Hebrew, from a Hebrew perspective, the majority of the surviving copies were written in Greek. These were then translated into English and other languages, losing much of the original significance. With that said, let's continue.

The Messiah is the anointed of God. A King of Israel or a High Priest would be anointed using oil that was considered holy. There have been many arguments that Yeshua was never officially anointed as one would have expected, however in the case of Yeshua there are several witnesses to his anointing.

The first witness is in Matthew 3:16, a second in Luke 4:18-21 with his proclamation of the fulfillment of the passage from the scroll of the prophet he had read from, a third in Luke 7:46, a fourth in Matthew 26:6 and a final one at his burial in John 19:39. He was anointed both by man and by God and certainly more than once.

If we look at the time the Magi/Wise men had come to find him after his birth, we see also that they had brought Myrrh as a gift. The only purpose for this was for his anointing as King. They even said that they had come to find the one born King of Israel.

Furthermore, he is our High Priest (Cohen Gadol). Paul/Shaul declares in Hebrews 4:14 (HRB), "We have therefore a great High Priest who has passed through the heavens, Yahshua, the Son of YAHWEH, let us remain firm in His faith."

With this I think we have a good understanding of Yeshua as the Messiah. There are several prophecies of his birth, death and resurrection. The Tanakh speaks on several instances of a coming Messiah that would be King. We see him in his first coming in the Gospels. Today, at this point in time, we are in expectation of his second coming, also prophesied of, as described in Revelation, and other books of the Bible.

Yeshua the Messiah is King, High Priest and anointed of God. He is the Torah, as we have already seen; the Way, the Truth and the Life. It is also important for this chapter to mention again that no one comes to the Father but by Him.

So what would an anti-messiah look like?

The title of this chapter mentions an anti-torah as well as an anti-messiah. The two are one and the same. You cannot have one without the other.

"Anti" is defined as "opposed to; against." It's the idea of the enemy of something; an antagonist to a protagonist. Most would be familiar with the term "anti-christ." Most picture this as a single man, satan or a system that is put in place. All are true.

1 John 4:3 states this:

> "And every spirit who does not confess that Yeshua the Messiah has come in the flesh is not of God, and this is the spirit of the Anti-messiah, of whom you have heard that it comes.

Now it is in the
world   already."
(HNV)

The entire book of 1 John is a must read when dealing with this topic. If you read on in 5:3, it also states:

"For this is the love
of God, that we keep
his commandments.
His commandments
are not grievous."
(HNV)

Some translations say, "His commandments are not a burden."

It seems apparent to me that an anti-messiah would be someone who does not follow Torah. Considering the state of the world from the beginning until now, this could be any person on the planet. Remember, he said it is the "spirit of anti-messiah." A spirit can be classified as different things. The Hebrew word is "Ruach" which can be of the mind, spirit or wind/breath. It is more popularly accepted as "spirit" but also relates to the "breath" of the Almighty. "Holy Spirit" in Hebrew is "Ruach Hakodesh."

As followers, we are to adhere to the Torah of the Almighty. So what about a person who does not? If we, who follow Torah, are full of the Ruach of God, what spirit is it of for those who do not follow Torah? Perhaps then it would be the spirit of anti-messiah? Some may claim that this is an issue of morality, which is man's word for defining right from wrong. Much of the Torah deals with "morality" as we refer to it. Now looking more into the Torah, we see certain practices we should do and commands against certain practices that should be avoided.

34

For the sake of simplicity I will use the command to Keep the Sabbath. It is the fourth command given in Exodus/Shemot 20. The instructions were to remember the Sabbath day, keep it holy and do no work on it. The Sabbath day is the seventh day of the week. Further instructions found in the prophets also present the prohibition against buying, selling or trading on this day. If these are the instructions given by the Almighty, then why not do as He commands? Many believe that they are no longer required to keep the Torah. So then, their decision is that they reject the Almighty's instructions. They will do work on the Sabbath, do no rest and will possibly even suggest that the Almighty's seventh day Sabbath was changed to the first day of the week instead, even though there is no evidence that the Almighty said this at all. A regular argument that it was changed is that they see the Apostles congregating or meeting on the first day, therefore, we should too. This however is a very weak argument and sounds more like following examples of others rather than the Almighty or the Messiah. This is anti-Torah; to be opposed to or against the instructions of the Almighty. Though this is a hot topic for many, I will continue on.

A person who is anti-torah is adverse to it. They have no love for it, find it irrelevant for today or perhaps even consider it evil. This is a sobering thought that perhaps today's believers, who teach against the Torah, have been given to the great deception that God's ways are no longer to be man's ways, since the resurrection of Yeshua. Scripture, I believe, disagrees with these teachings, especially in light of 1 John 5:3.

Consider also the term "satan." This is a Hebrew word which means "adversary." In Matthew 16, Yeshua is telling his disciples that he must go into Jerusalem to suffer many things (foretold to be and fulfilled). Peter objects to this and Yeshua's reply is, "(V. 23) Go behind me, adversary! You are an offense to

Me, for you do not think of the things of YHVH, but the things of men."

The Messiah kept the Torah. He lived it out and fulfilled it as was foretold of his life on earth. He also says himself, in Matthew 5, in the same teaching as Matthew 7, that he, "did not come to do away with (or destroy) the Torah but to fulfill (or complete) it."

I have to make a very harsh statement here. It is not a popular thing to say and may even be considered politically incorrect. However, I must say it.

A person who does not follow the Torah is quite possibly of the spirit of anti-messiah and is anti-torah.

In Acts 15:19-21 (NJB), James (Ya'akov) spoke and said, "My verdict is, then, that instead of making things more difficult for gentiles who turn to God, we should send them a letter telling them merely to abstain from anything polluted by idols, from illicit marriages, from the meat of strangled animals and from blood. For Moses has always had his preachers in every town and is read aloud in the synagogues every Sabbath."

The apostles/emissaries had a counsel. Their analysis was that every new believer should hear about and learn the Torah in the synagogues every Sabbath. Initially, they were to abstain from the things listed in this passage, but, would eventually learn more about the Torah in their weekly synagogues. The Torah was also referred to as "Moses" or "Moshe" since he was the one known to have written it down onto scrolls.

To my eyes, it seemed a very merciful thing to ease them into the Torah. There are many commands and laws given throughout the Torah and can be a task to take on all at once, but, it is fair to instruct a new believer to be moral and healthy from the beginning.

36

Orders of the Priesthoods

A popular question that arises when talking about keeping Torah is, "Why don't we continue animal sacrifices?" I'll answer this in a small yet profound way.

When the Torah was first given, we were also given instructions under the Levitical Priesthood. The Levites were to take care of all the sacrifices and fire offerings. This was to occur in and around the Temple, or Tabernacle.

When Yeshua came to fulfill the Torah, one of the things he fulfilled was the sacrificial system. He gave his own life as a perfect sacrifice. At the same time, we were placed under the order of Melchizedek. This is a very ancient order that predates the Levitical order. The Levitical order was very important in it's time, but we are now under a greater order of the Melchizedek. Yeshua is the High Priest of the order of Melchizedek, which in Hebrew means, "King of Righteousness."

The Levitical Priesthood was in charge of the temple. They are better known as the "Levites." They would perform the fire offerings, sacrifices and were permitted in and around the Temple. The duties were placed in their care.

Yeshua prophesied that the second Temple would be destroyed (Matthew 24) and that prophecy came to pass between 68 CE and 70 CE (Common Era). Since the Temple was no more, the Levitical Priesthood was of no effect anymore. However, 1 Corinthians 6:19 says that our bodies are the Temple within which the Ruach HaKodesh/Holy Spirit abides. Our High Priest, Yeshua, of the order of the Melchizedek Priesthood, maintains and performs all the duties for this Temple. You can read more about this in Hebrews 7. The first mention of Melchizedek can be found in Genesis/Barashite 14. There is also a prophecy concerning Yeshua becoming the Melchizedek Priest in Psalm/Tehelim 110.

In summary, we are in the world but not to be of the world (John 15). We are called to be a peculiar people (1 Peter 2:9) and a holy/kadosh nation unto Yah (Exodus 19:6). In my experience, no group of people looks like that of those who follow Torah. We are saved by grace through Yeshua but those who love God keep His Commandments/Torah (1 John 5:3). It is our Law, our creed and our instructions. It is the Way, the Truth and the Life of the believer and follower of Yeshua the Messiah and His Father. To reject or denounce the Father's and His Messiah's ways (The Torah) is to be anti-messiah and anti-torah and such a person is, "you who practice lawlessness." We should be imitators of the Messiah, the Torah-made-man, and not the lawless one (2 Thessalonians 2:8).

The definition of sin comes from 1 John 3:4 which states, "Everyone who keeps sinning is violating Torah — indeed, sin is violation of Torah." (CJB) Other versions use words and phrases such as "wickedness," "transgression of the law" and "lawlessness" (KJV, NJB, HNV).

Lawlessness is to be without Torah.

Chapter 4 – Yeshua's Fulfillment of the Seven Feasts of Yah

I believe we have established that the Torah is an integral part of a believer's life. There are so many different parts that we could examine, and I believe every believer should regularly study the Torah. However, for the topic of this book we will have to restrain ourselves and focus more on point.

There are seven Feast days given by the almighty in the Torah, four in the spring and three in the fall. There are particularly important chapters to look at when one wants to study on them such as Leviticus/ Vayikra 23, Numbers/Bamidbar 29 and Deuteronomy/Devarim 16.

You may be asking 'what is so important about these days?' The answer is EVERTHING! Any time the Almighty makes mention of something more than once in Scripture, it is of great importance. And the Feast days are mentioned more than twice.

The Feast Days were, and are, days to remember something historical for Israel. They are also prophetic forshadowings of "things to come." Passover, or in Hebrew "Pesach," was a remembrance of when the death angel swept through Egypt to claim the firstborn of every family (Exodus/Shemot 11). The Hebrews were instructed to sacrifice a lamb, eat it and place it's blood on their doorposts. When death saw this it was to "pass over" them and spare their firstborn. From then on, this day has been celebrated annually in the first month of the Biblical calendar in remembrance of this event. However, unknown at that time, this was also a foretelling of the coming Messiah who would be our ultimate "Passover Lamb," fulfilling this Feast in every way.

Historically, Yeshua fulfilled all four of the Spring Feasts of Yah. These Feasts consist of Passover (Pesach), Unleavened Bread (Chag ha-Matzot), Firstfruits (Chag ha-Bikkurim) which is also the Feast of the Harvest, and Pentecost (Shavuot). Some believe, and so do I, that these Feast Day prophecies were fulfilled by Yeshua on the exact days and each specific requirement of these Feasts were fulfilled at the precise moment they were to be observed by the Hebrews throughout Israel.

Yeshua is described as the "Passover Lamb" (1 Corinthians 5:7), having carried our sins away as the leaven is removed from our homes (1 Peter 2:24) and was the first fruits from among those who have fallen asleep (1 Corinthians 15:20). Then on Shavuot, a celebration of the day we received the Torah, we received the Ruach Hakodesh/Holy Spirit and the Torah/Law was written on our hearts (Romans 2:14-15) as it was prophesied in Jeremiah/Yermiyahu 31:33. We now wait for the second coming and the final fulfillment of the three Fall Feasts.

Yeshua explained it well in Luke 4:18-19 as he began reading from a scroll:

> "The Spirit of the LORD is upon Me, Because He has anointed Me to preach the gospel to the poor; He has sent Me to heal the

brokenhearted, to
proclaim liberty
to the captives and
recovery of sight to
the blind, to set at
liberty those who are
oppressed; to
proclaim the
acceptable year of
the LORD."
(NKJV)

He then ended in the middle of the passage, because he came first as a Suffering Servant. The next part of the scroll he was reading from, which was Isaiah/Yeshayahu 61, would continue to say, "And the day of vengeance of our God," which describes his role as a Conquering King. This will take place as the fulfillment of the prophecy of the Fall Feasts and this is described in more detail in the Revelation of John/Yochanon.

The Fall Feasts consist of the Day of Trumpets (Yom Teruah), the Day of Atonement (Yom Kippur) and the Feast of Tabernacles (Sukkot).

Because these Fall Feasts are yet to be fulfilled by Yeshua, there are a lot of opinions on how he will actually fulfill them. The information leading to those opinions are mostly derived from different parts of the New Testament/B'rit Chadesha. Through my studies in Matthew 24 and Revelation 6, the following is my interpretation of how the Fall Feasts will be fulfilled by Yeshua.

These will begin on Yom Teruah with him gathering his people unto himself as told in 1 Thess. 4:16-17 which says,

"For the
Lord himself shall
descend from heaven

41

with a shout, with the voice of the archangel, and with the trump of God: and the dead in Christ shall rise first: Then we which are alive and remain shall be caught up together with them in the clouds, to meet the Lord in the air: and so shall we ever be with the Lord." (KJV)

This will lead into Yom Kippur when there will be Judgment of those of us who are gathered. Judgment will be of our works and the Almighty's observing of the atoning blood of Yeshua upon us. However, leading up to this day the people on the Earth will be going through a terrible time that will last for 10 days. This will be the pouring out of Yah's wrath upon the whole Earth.

Finally, Sukkot will be when the marriage supper of the Lamb and on the Last Great Day the 1,000 year reign will begin. It is also believed to be the birthday of Yeshua because He "dwelt/tabernacled among us" (John 1).

The Hebrew term for these Feasts is "Moedim" meaning "appointed times." If God sets an appointed time for us to meet with Him, like on the Sabbath, and we decide to either not observe this time or to do it another time, do you think we would miss Him? Wouldn't it make more sense to meet with Him on HIS appointed time? Should you be astonished that He didn't meet with you on your time? Just something to consider.

I would also like to point out that these are not called the "Feasts of the Jews". In the Torah, they are called "Feasts of the LORD".

In summary, as I hope you see, the Torah is not dead. If Yeshua is the Torah-made-man and he lives, then the Feast Days of the Torah hold such an importance and should still be observed in today's time. If He fulfilled the Spring Feasts precisely and completely during his first coming, would he not do the same with the Fall Feasts during his second coming? Not only are they to help us remember what has passed, but also to look to the future as Yeshua is the hope we strive for. HalleluYAH!

Chapter 5 – The Commission of Yeshua/The Will of the Father

I consider the preceding chapters as information that is "in case you didn't know." To bring my fellow brothers and sisters up to speed, and catch us all up on the same page that we should all be on without having gone into too lengthy of detail, but just enough to stir the curiosity. Hopefully, they have been a call to dust off that old Bible you haven't touched in a while, or perhaps to go into a study, objectively, to test the Scriptures against what I have touched on so far.

Before I began writing this book, I was involved in public speaking at different places. Any time I spoke to a new congregation, and often times I'd repeat myself to a familiar one, I would say to never take anything I or anyone else said without testing it. Always study it out, ask the hard questions and consult with the great Teacher himself (Our Mount Moriah).

We now come to a place where I believe the answers will become more apparent. It took me years of sleepless nights wrestling and struggling with these truths. I finally discovered the answers I had been looking for, even though they were there all along. I hope that what you are about to read will help to put the light back on the right path for you, or perhaps to encourage you to stay on the right path and for you to know how to speak with or help others around you who are searching in the dark.

As I look around at the world today, I see on the news and I hear in conversations I have with others; the world needs the message of the Messiah. Before they can receive that message, the disciples of Messiah (you and me) need to stay focused on what that message is. Too often, I see fellow believers, myself included, getting "Off Topic," arguing over this doctrine or that. This book is my call to get back ON topic. The world needs this message, and we are the messengers.

The Will of the Father

This statement is heavy to me. Not burdensome, but full of importance. Let's read Yeshua's words in Matthew 28:18-20.

"Yeshua came to them and spoke to them, saying, 'All authority has been given to me in heaven and on earth.

Go, and make disciples of all nations, immersing them in the name of the Father and of the Son and of the Holy Spirit, teaching them to observe all things that I commanded you. Behold, I am with you always, even to the end of

This has been called by many, "The Great Commission." The word "Disciples" comes from the Hebrew word "Talmidim." It is a plural version of Talmid, which means "Student." You can consider that if you call yourself a follower of Yeshua, then you are also calling yourself a student, disciple or apprentice of Yeshua. What Yeshua is saying here, is to go and make others like the ones he was speaking to - Talmidim - who later would become known as Apostles or Emissaries (special messengers). He wanted them to deliver the same message that he had taught his entire ministry - the message of the Kingdom.

What is the message of the Kingdom? I would like to submit that it is this, that in the beginning, the Almighty created us and gave us all free will to choose His way or to rebel against Him. We chose to rebel. Since this initial act of sin, which by definition is to break the Torah commands (1 John 3:4), we were separated from the Almighty. He however had a plan of reconciliation, not wanting that we should perish. Throughout history He proved His power over and over again. He made a covenant with the people, any who would listen, "If you obey My commands, I will bless you." He saved them from oppression, danger and their very own sins; all this and more. He even made His small chosen people into a great Nation; however, they again and again rebelled against Him and His Torah. After many judgments and corrections, this eventually lead to the Almighty divorcing His people because of their adultery against Him as they followed after their own lusts and ways, which broke the covenant He had made with them (Jeremiah 3:8).

However, He promised a Savior. He would come and wash away their sins with his own blood. He did come, and his name was Yeshua. He lived a perfect life in accordance to the Torah and

46

Will of the Father. He fulfilled every prophecy told of him for his first coming as a suffering servant. His death and resurrection brought the people of the Creator and the Creator Himself back into relationship, much like a marriage contract. Through Yeshua's sacrifice, which annulled the debt of our sin, and his resurrection, which renewed the marriage contract, we were saved by the grace of the Almighty. The covenant of death was broken and the covenant of life was renewed, "If you obey my commands I will bless you." He also gave a promise; that Yeshua would return for us, abolish all evil from the world and we would reign with him for eternity.

So then, we are saved by grace through Yeshua's death and resurrection, and as a result, we show the Creator our love by keeping His Torah. One day we will be in a perfect society with Him and the Messiah and all other Talmidim.

This is, of course, my way of telling this great Message. Others like to tell it their own way, which I have no problem with as long as they are delivering His message. However, the point isn't only in delivering the Message; it's keeping the Message in our walk; in how we live our daily lives. You have to keep Torah to preach Torah.

If you recall back in Matthew 7 when Yeshua said he would say, "Depart from me, you who practice lawlessness," he was talking to those who may do certain things (like casting out demons) but they perhaps did not walk the Torah walk, nor hold in their hearts the most important part of all; Love.

"Whoever does not love does not know God, because God is love." (1 John 4) Why is it important to love? Yeshua explained it this way in Matthew 22:37-40, "'You shall love the Lord your God with all your heart, with all your soul, and with all your mind.' This is the first and great commandment. And the second is like it: 'You shall love your neighbor as yourself.' On these two commandments hang all the Torah and the Prophets." These words were not just Yeshua's, but he was repeating what the Torah said in Deuteronomy/Devarim 6 and in Leviticus/Vayikra 19:18.

This tells me one thing; Love is everything. This is why I like to call it the "Torah of Love." If there is no love, then what is there to hang on to? The Torah hangs on love, therefore if you remove love the Torah falls apart! Perhaps these people who were told to depart did these things but did not have love? I hope you are seeing the complexity of the issue that was presented in chapter 1.

I now want to examine something else Yeshua said in the commission. He said to make Talmidim, "Immersing them in the name of the Father, the Son and the Holy Spirit." Some versions say "Baptising" which is from the Hebrew "Mikveh."

Some believe this is a Trinitarian statement. I think otherwise. Consider the wording of the statement. It very well could be in reference to the Mikveh, however, I like to think it may also mean to immerse them into the NAME of the Father, Son and Ruach HaKodesh. What is the Name? Why is that so important? On to the next chapter!

Chapter 6 – The Name

The name of the Creator is a hot topic where there is hardly any agreement on its proper use. This chapter is my personal belief in the Name with clarification of my reasoning.

I have talked about and shown the meaning behind the Messiah's name. There is a possibility of the inclusion of the Creator's name. Many of the prophets in the Tanakh have the poetic shortened version of the Name, Yah, in their own names such as Isaiah (Yeshayahu, meaning Yah is Salvation), Elijah (Eliyahu, meaning My El/God is Yah) and Zechariah (Zecharyah, meaning Yah Remembers). Remember also that every Hebrew name has a meaning.

If you look at Joshua's name in Hebrew, Yehoshua, you will notice the shortened version of the Name is pronounced differently, Yeh instead of Yah. Names in Scripture involving the Creator's Name never appear to have a "Yah" sound when the Name is at the beginning, at least, not in Hebrew. This is the first part of my reason for not using the version "Yahweh" or any other version starting with "Yah." I, however, do not cringe if others use it. Many people I know use this version, but I choose not to. That is their walk, not mine!

I now want to examine three Hebrew words – Haya (היה), Hove (הווה) and Yihye (יהיה). These mean "was, is, and will be."

Now look at the name of the Creator in Hebrew – יהוה (Yod-Hey-Vav-Hey, read right to left) with all the exact same letters. Now I will show the name with the vowels and consonants added – יְהֹוָה - with the vowels shva, cholam and kamatz, this suggests the pronunciation "Yehovah." Though I used to call the Almighty "Yahweh," upon learning this version of the Name I started calling Him "Yehovah."

There is a scroll called the "Allepo Codex." It was scribed by men who are popularly believed to have known the proper pronunciation of the Name. However, because of the ban on the use of the Name, they were forbidden to write the vowel pointings with the name. But about 50 times, they seem to maybe have accidentally written them anyway, in the form I showed in the previous paragraph. Was it a mistake? Maybe. Or it could have been planned. No one truly knows. But even so, some have also adopted the possibility of the pronunciation being "Yehowah" or "Yehuah." This is because if the Vav has a dot above it, this makes the Vav a Cholam (i) and the V sound becomes silent. The cholam though does not require the Vav to be present and can simply be a dot above the word and between two letters.

This is highly debated and controversial. As I have mentioned already, some believe the name "Too Holy" to pronounce. Others believe in several other pronunciations. I however like to focus on the meaning that He "was, is and will be." The Almighty spoke to Moshe/Moses and said to tell Pharaoh of Himself, "אֶהְיֶה אֲשֶׁר הָאֶהְיֶ" (Ehyeh Asher Ehyeh), translated as "I am that I am" by some, and "I will be what I will be" by others which is most accurate. I have also heard many argue that the version "Yehovah" should not be used because of the sound "Hovah," which means "a ruin; disaster." I think this is a poor argument because you can hear "Rah," meaning "evil," in "Torah." Torah, as already explained, means "Instructions." Does

50

this then mean that the Torah is evil? I think not. Therefore it is a poor argument for not using this version.

What is in a name? As I have mentioned before, every Hebrew name has a meaning, and it appears to my eyes and ears that the Name of the Creator means to us that Yah is "Everywhere" and is "At all times." He is before us, above us, and all around us; what should we fear?

Read what the Creator has to say in Jeremiah 23:23-24 (HRB), "I Am an Elohim near by, says יְהֹוָה, and not an Elohim from afar. Or can a man hide himself in secret places so that I do not see him, says יְהֹוָה? Do I not fill the heavens and the earth, says יְהֹוָה?"

First I'd like to point out that you just read Hebrew! Next, notice the use of His own name three times in this statement in referring to where He is and how close to us He is. In time, he "was, is and will be," in location he also, "was here, is here and will be here," and at the same time he "was there, is there and will be there." See how great the name of Yehovah is?!

In summary, I want to share a few passages with you.

Joel 2:32a, "And everyone who calls on the name of Yehovah will be saved..."

Isaiah 42:8, "I am Yehovah; that is My name; and I will not give My glory to another, nor My praise to engraved images."

I also want to encourage you to read the Shema (or Sh'ma, Hebrew meaning Hear/Listen and Obey) in Deuteronomy 6. Remember that anytime you see LORD or GOD in all capital letters, this is where Moshe and the Prophets originally wrote the Name of El, Yehovah (יְהֹוָה).

Remember also, that anytime you say the Name or see it in Scripture that Proverbs 18:10 says, "The name of יְהֹוָה is a tower of strength, the righteous run into it and is set on high," meaning that He is with you always. HalleluYAH! (Praise, be unto YAH!)

Chapter 7 – From Aleph to Tav

This is the last chapter of this book. If it hasn't been clear so far, I want to call out in plain sight what the point of this book is. It is a call to do exactly what it is we were called to do, "Make Disciples!"

Our world is sick and dying. It needs healing. It needs salvation. It needs a Savior.

The purpose of creation is to have relationship with the Creator (and with one another) and that He is exalted on high. Mankind has fallen far from this purpose. It was allowed, but with certain freewill choices come consequences.

Without invoking the fear of hell, for me, the worst part of being separate from the Creator is, being separate from the Creator. If He is Life, Love and every good thing, how could I or anyone else ever bear to be apart from Him? Are these not the very things we all search for in our lives? Aside from that, is it not to have purpose and meaning?

We, Talmidim, do have purpose and meaning, and that is to get the word out. It is delivering Love to the nations and communities and in Love, making Talmidim of Love.

We spread Life and Truth. There can be nothing more than the Message of Yah that can bring us everything our soul and spirit has ever longed for.

Yah says something very interesting in Revelation 1:8, "I am the Aleph and the Tav, the Beginning and the Ending, says Adonai Yah, the One who is, and who was, and who is coming, the Almighty."

Aleph is the first letter of the Hebrew alphabet (or alephbet). Tav is the last letter. The Hebrew alephbet is very interesting to learn and holds many deeper meanings than simply being a language. But in general, He is saying He is everything. He is the Beginning and the Ending. He then repeats Haya, Hove, Yihye.

Throughout this process, I have done my own praying and studying. I have also had others pray for this book and me while undertaking this task. And this is what I believe to be the most important thing I can say thus far in my life. The point I am trying to make is in this final summary.

We were put on this planet for a purpose. The Almighty Yehovah created us. He has never said of His own work, "Oops." He does not make mistakes. You are not a mistake. We were fearfully and wonderfully made (Psalm/Tehelim 139). We are capable of so much; beings that can create and build, or destroy and tear down. The Almighty gave us freewill. We have choices to make and I want to encourage you to choose life that you might live. "This day I call the heavens and the earth as witnesses against you that I have set before you life and death, blessings and curses. Now choose life, so that you and your children may live...," (Deuteronomy/Devarim 30:19).

If you choose life (Yehovah is your life, Deuteronomy/ Devarim 30:20), then there is a way for you to live. Live by the

54

Torah of Yehovah and follow His Messiah Yeshua who is also life (John 14:6), as one of his Talmidim.

If this is the life you have chosen and the way you have chosen to believe in, then I want you to pay very close attention to what I now have to say.

We are a holy people; separate from the world, but in it nonetheless. So what do we do here? We live the Kingdom!

The Kingdom of Yah's citizens, us, the called and chosen, are to live holy lives before the Creator and amongst the potential chosen of Yah, as their example.

The Message we have to deliver, has in the past, had many killed. It is such a powerful Word that it tears down worldly and corrupt kingdoms; personal or governmental. But be encouraged, your reward will be great!

Yeshua walked this Earth around 2000 years ago and still today his message, which is the message of the Kingdom of Yah, has survived. The Torah was written around 5000 years ago and has also survived. He has had many carry that message and deliver it to the ears of people in all walks of life. From kings to politicians to average people working average jobs or homeless wanderers; He has spoken to them all through people like you and me. It's now our time and we have one shot at this, one life to get it right and do what we were commissioned to do. So let's do it!

Study to show yourself approved; always be ready to give an answer for the reason you believe! Know the message Yeshua taught and teach it also! Live it, breath it, speak it and be true to it! Worshipping the Almighty and blessing His name is shown through how we live our lives.

Many believers today have gotten so far off topic. We argue about when the rapture will occur, if the Trinity is a true doctrine, whether we are in the tribulation already or not; but that isn't what we were told to focus on. We were told to deliver the good news and make disciples and to live the life. That is what I submit we do.

Of what importance is the rapture? Does knowing its true timing bring salvation? Does it bring redemption to a fallen people? I'm not saying it's wrong to discuss these things, but the issue I see is that we have been focusing on these topics rather than the central one. This is especially off topic when we are talking to someone of another denomination or belief.

"Teshuva" is a Hebrew word that means to "return." Repentance was the message of John the Immerser/Baptist. When he was killed, Yeshua picked up that same message and delivered it just as John did. Repent! Teshuva! Return to the ways of Yah! That is our message. But what does it look like or sound like to speak this message?

Yeshua had a following of people and he would sit and speak with them about the Torah and the fulfillment of it. As priest of my home I am to ensure that my daughter and wife know this message and learn it well. But I also have neighbors and friends and other family members I have to speak with, and this can be a difficult task. Many get discouraged when speaking to someone who believes in Jesus but not the Torah, or an atheist or a pagan. What do we do?

We tell them the message and are there to answer any questions. I do not believe we should beat them over the head with it, but we should still tell them the message if they are willing to let us. And, of course, always in love!

I'm not talking about holding signs up on the street corners or handing out tracts; I mean talking with a person one-on-one and heart-to-heart. You don't have to reach out to the masses, you can speak to one person at a time, and if they choose this life as you have, then for them it means eternal life, and another disciple has begun their journey. Living in this world, but not of it, is a narrow path to walk. The Torah is our guide and light. Keeping Torah will feed the flame of our light to help others find the path.

The focus should be on Yeshua and helping others understand the proper perspective of who he is. He is the Word of Yah. He lived the life of Torah and fulfilled his part as Messiah and Savior. He died to take our sins away and resurrected so we may have relationship with the Father. He will come again to bring us to the Father that we may live eternally with Him in a perfect way.

Questions may come from those willing to accept this message. "What do I do now?" "Where do I go from here?"

Answer them by encouraging them to do what is right; to walk a clean and holy walk according to Torah. Then tell them to study the Torah, the first five books of the Bible as often as they can and learn the ways of the Almighty because this teaches what is right and wrong.

More questions may come like, "Should I start animal sacrifices?" Then explain the sacrifice of Yeshua was the perfection and fulfillment of the Torah sacrifices, putting an end to animal sacrifices. You can explain the Feasts and why we observe them and the order of Melchizedek.

They may ask, "What should I tell others?" Their willingness to tell others is great, and shouldn't be discouraged. I would tell them to first learn the Scriptures, live them and when they feel comfortable enough to share the message of the Scriptures, to do so. Tell them not to be discouraged when they are mocked or made fun of because there will be times when they are. Tell them to remember that what they now believe is a message that men of Yah have died for, so that we may know the Truth.

There will be some who don't care about the message. They may reject it and mock it, but that is their choice. We have to respect their decision. If they are willing to discuss their reasons with you, be willing to listen and to share your reasons as well. A friendly conversation between opposing views never hurts!

Brothers and sisters, Yeshua died for this message, and its fulfillment. His followers were killed because they held onto its hope and delivered the message so that the Kingdom of Yah may grow and prosper and that the people may have hope for life and salvation. He has chosen people like you and me to tell the world about His love and His great Way and the hope we have in Yeshua that there will be a day that all pain and suffering and corruption is done away with. There will one day be a King that will rule greater than any other king ever has before. The people will be well cared for, and that King will rule with righteousness! That's our King in Heaven!

It will require faith and trust. Some days it may rain, others it will pour, but some days it will shine. This is all part of being one of His own. Though there are many dangers and troubles, we serve an ALMIGHTY God in Heaven who is with us at all times.

I want to encourage you now to read the Scriptures for yourself. This book is merely a starting point, a stepping stone or a rekindling of a flame gone out. We need to learn or relearn the Words of our God and find our willingness to get back into the world and deliver this message at all costs.

We have been given His Ruach, His Spirit to accomplish this task. The very breath of the Almighty is within us, all we have to do is breathe.

One day, maybe today, you will find the courage to go and speak about the Torah's significance with church leaders who teach against it. I believe we know well enough, that the deception of the adversary/satan has snuck its way into congregations all throughout the nations; messages that say "Christ is the end of the law!" If this message is being improperly portrayed as the truth, shouldn't we be out there telling the Truth that Yeshua is not the end of the Law/Torah, but rather IS the Law/Torah?

Confrontation is never easy, but it is important to do when necessary. Yeshua taught us that if a lamb strays we must go and bring it back into the fold. It's so important that he had the need to tell us to do it. When we see someone stray, we should go after them and guide them in love to return/teshuva to the Almighty and His Torah. Reason with the "Sanhedrin" of our day.

Immerse yourself into the Father and His Word. Know the Truth, internalize it and allow it to be written on your heart. Live His Way and denounce your own. There will be times when you are given the opportunity to share the message of the Kingdom, and when you do, you will be empowered by the Ruach to speak it. But remember to do so in love and humility. Our sword is not a physical and violent one, but the Word of God that causes devils to flee. It cuts to the heart and can expose every lie of the enemy. Let His Word be your guiding light and your bread of life. Trust in Him and He will guide you. Not only will your treasures in Heaven be great, but you will have lived a life worthy of Yeshua, saying something wonderful and rich.

I believe we will hear words similar to those spoken in one of Yeshua's parables in Matthew 25, "Well done, good and faithful

59

servant. You have been faithful over a few things; I will set you over many things. Enter into the joy of your lord."

And so I end with this, from Matthew 7:24-27 which says:

"Then everyone who hears these Words from Me, and does them, I will compare him to a wise man who built his house on the rock; and the rain came down, and the floods came up, and the winds blew, and fell against that house; but it did not fall, for it had been founded on the rock. And everyone who hears these Words of Mine, and who does not do them, he shall be compared to a foolish man who built his house on the sand; and the rain came down, and the floods came up, and the winds blew and beat against that house; and it fell, and great was the collapse of it."

Special Thanks

I would like to extend a special thank you to my friends and family that have helped in putting this book together. I also want to thank my wife and daughter for helping me with the beautiful picture on the front cover. I especially want to thank the Almighty Creator for His great influence in my life and for helping me walk His path. HalleluYAH!

I would also like to extend an invitation to the readers to join me on the following networks:

www.michaeldsofer.com
www.facebook.com/hebraicperspectives
www.twitter.com/Mihaal86
www.youtube.com/mihaal86

If you would like to contact me, you may do so at:

MichaelDSofer@outlook.com

Shalom/Peace

www.ingramcontent.com/pod-product-compliance
Lightning Source LLC
Chambersburg PA
CBHW060724030426
42337CB00017B/3003